WITS,
WISDOMS,
AND
WONDERS...

To Sharron and Barry,

All the best and hope

you enjoy!

10-1-20

FROM THE AUTHOR OF

FUNNY CONVERSATIONS WITH GOD
– AN UNCALLED-FOR DIALOGUE

ROCK BOTTOM, THEN UP AGAIN
– AND OTHER SPIRITUAL ESSAYS

Wits, Wisdoms, and Wonders...

For Navigating This Thing Called Life

DUNN NEUGEBAUER

MOUNTAIN ARBOR
PRESS

MOUNTAIN ARBOR
PRESS
Alpharetta, GA

ISBN: 978-1-63183-903-0 - Paperback
eISBN: 978-1-63183-904-7 - Epub
eISBN: 978-1-63183-905-4 - mobi

Library of Congress Control Number: 2020912975

Printed in the United States of America   0 7 1 4 2 0

♾This paper meets the requirements of ANSI/NISO Z39.48-1992 (Permanence of Paper)

Author photos by Julie Fennell

How This
Happened...

A few years ago, a parent – with a kid about to graduate high school – asked me if I'd send a note to the future honoree, something nice. Nowadays, people accomplish the same thing with a short video, and it takes 30 seconds or less. You just point and shoot, hit 'send' and voila, all finished.

Back then, though, email was the thing so – under the influence of either boredom or one too many glasses of wine – I boldly faced my computer. What do you tell a graduate? I was 55-years-old or so at the time, what had I learned? What would I have told an 18, or even a 22-year-old me about to move away from home?

In short, the assignment intrigued me – made me think, scratch my head, pace the floor. What would I have wanted to read after leaving high school in 1978, or college in 1982? What wits, wisdoms and wonders would've propelled me forward, kept me from a world of dung, or at the very least, made me laugh?

Realizing almost no one wants to read a long email – okay, NO ONE does – I quickly thought of 20 or so bullet points, hit 'send' and went back to my bad sitcoms. And that, I thought, was the end of that.

A year later, however, while freezing my butt off in carpool, that graduate drove through to pick up her younger sister. Rolling down the window despite the chill, she told me she'd not only read my notes, but kept them minimalized on her computer, referred to them often.

Being a writer, hearing that someone actually READS your stuff is a major boost, having them "refer" to it and "read it often" is a like pitching a no-hitter and hitting a grand slam in the same game.

Filled with confidence, I proceeded to send out – unsolicited – a similar email to the seniors each year. Though many may have deleted it on the spot, I'd like to think many of the kids read them; were perhaps nudged just a little if not a lot.

In moving on, soon the list grew and kept growing; I'd find myself jogging when I'd think of one or two, then search everywhere for a pencil or a pen. Often, I would jot the key words on my hand where I'd remember it later.

So, here's the result of notes on napkins, words on hands, wits scrawled on the inside pages of books or paper plates or anything I could find. It was, and still is, a fun project, but it's more than that. It's bullet points of lessons learned, triumphs and failures, getting the girl and not even getting close, winning big but losing even worse, daring and chickening out.

In other words, life. After all, sometimes the best way to gain wisdoms is by making mistakes – both big and small. Hopefully reading at least some of these will hit home, make you think, maybe make your own list for somebody else.

If nothing else, it's nice to put what you've gained, lost, learned, and loved on paper – right out there front and center – for you to see and others to learn from.

Hope you enjoy. And I'm sorry for this long "email." Still, I must admit, I hope you minimalize it on your computer, refer to it often, think about some of these long and hard.

Have a great day; have a great life; and, as always, thanks for listening…

Dunn Neugebauer

Try not to fall in love too fast, and never believe a guy when he's on his third drink.

* * *

Approach with confidence
or don't approach at all.

* * *

If you can't find the road less traveled,
create it.

* * *

Remember: It is love that makes the world go round, but it's gratitude that keeps it afloat.

If you're in someone else's girlfriend's room after dark, make sure you have an escape route. Almost getting thrown out of a 3rd floor window wasn't very fun.

● ● ●

ALWAYS wear something under your toga. This can be embarrassing if you don't – though of course I'm reporting this "for a friend."

● ● ●

Not only can nice people finish first, but they can sleep like a baby after doing it.

● ● ●

Remember: Your focus is your magnet.

Never trust an "expert" when it comes to the stock market. There's no such thing.

● ● ●

Three things when preparing for anything:
1) take care of everything you can take care of;
2) put karma on your side, and;
3) do your best.

● ● ●

If you get dumped, don't act like a jerk about it. They need to see you at your BEST, not your worst. This makes them wonder if they made the right move.

And on the same subject, rejection equals
protection. In the long run,
you will be better off, whether it's a job,
a friend, or a romantic interest.

● ● ●

For you men out there: Your MAIN job in a
relationship is to make sure your woman
doesn't need another man. Period.

● ● ●

Pick your battles, and if you do engage in a
verbal dispute, make sure you know
what you're talking about.
Don't go into a battle of wits unarmed.

Speaking of, never interfere when women are planning a wedding. Sticking your head in a weed eater might be a better option.

● ● ●

Either wait tables or referee some type of sporting event at some point in your life. It will help your perspective.

● ● ●

Never throw a penalty flag at a hot woman on Bourbon Street. The hot boyfriend may not understand.

● ● ●

Speaking of Bourbon Street, always keep your wallet in your FRONT pocket.

You can find ways to find fault with every person or find ways to love them. If you choose love, you'll lead a far richer life.

• • •

Appreciate the little things.
Like cereal, a day without zits, a good cat nap, or finding a quarter on the ground.

• • •

Exercise in some form or fashion.
Being out of shape opens the door to sicknesses, cancers, and beyond.

Remember, sometimes it's okay to not be okay. After all, it's hard to get back on the horse when you're still in midair from falling.

● ● ●

Love as much as you can
and give thanks at every turn.

● ● ●

Learn when to shut up.

● ● ●

If you're ever running from security,
do NOT put a paper sack over your head
when doing it. You might run into a tree limb
and break your nose. Don't ask, I didn't.

During tough times, remember
these four words: This too shall pass.

   • • •

If you want to appear manly on your first
date, take all Bee Gees, John Denver,
and Air Supply tapes and hide them under
the car seat. Pretend you like Led Zeppelin.

   • • •

Go for a nature jog or walk
WITHOUT the headphones in.
The sounds of the wilderness can often do
you better than all of the above groups.

Keep all flattering emails you get and
start a 'gloat file.' On tough days,
these will help pull you through.

● ● ●

Talk to God as if He were your best friend.
I don't think you'll be punished for not
speaking in 'holier than thou' language.

● ● ●

Spend time around rivers, oceans, ponds,
and the like. After all, water is a mental eraser.

● ● ●

Incorporate balance in everything you do.
After all, even sunshine and water can kill if
you get too much.

Remember this line from the movie
"The Secret": Whatever you think about –
and thank about – you bring about.

● ● ●

According to google, some liquor drinks are
reported to be good for you. They're not.

● ● ●

Don't say 'yes' when someone asks if you
want the last piece, because they do.
They always do.

● ● ●

Remember: Sticks and stones can break your
bones, but your words CAN hurt as well. Say
something nice or muzzle yourself.

Learn how to read people's moods.
If they don't look like they want to talk to
you, then move the heck on.

* * *

Floss. You, and your wallet,
will be glad you did.

* * *

If you get off the plane and your knuckles are
white and your pants are brown, you
probably should reconsider becoming a
frequent flyer.

Don't complain, don't blame, and don't lie to
yourself. Growth comes from truth and
taking responsibility.

* * *

Keep a journal for at least a month. And if
someone asks to read it, tell them to buzz off.

* * *

Never sleep in a chair.
It's really not good for your back.

* * *

Showers rock, but every now and again,
soak in a hot bath.

And take a cold shower sometimes as well.
You can google the health benefits –
there are a lot of them.

● ● ●

Don't ask someone out on the phone,
do it to their face.
This makes it harder for them to say no.

● ● ●

Remember: Anybody can be nice when
they're around their friends and all is going
well. Even serial killers can do that.
How do you treat people on bad days?

Wear sunscreen, otherwise, you'll get burned physically now and financially later.

● ● ●

Never put anything on social media when angry or drunk.

● ● ●

When it seems like an acquaintance is about to ask for money, act like you're about to puke and then run to the bathroom. Good chance they'll be gone when you get back.

● ● ●

Don't believe it when people say, "he won't bite", "you can't miss it," "what could go wrong," or "just kidding."

If you don't want to get picked for the jury, do NOT crack a joke during the earlier questioning. Both sides like having a funny person in the courthouse if possible.

● ● ●

Get involved in social sports and activities, but don't take them so seriously! The officials aren't getting paid much, if at all, and your games probably aren't going to be on ESPN.

● ● ●

Before arguing with the opinionated souls of the world, ask yourself two questions: Is this really worth it? And does this REALLY matter?

When packing for college, don't forget a soap dish. Holding wet soap feels kind of gross.

● ● ●

Remember, there's no such thing as a sure thing. God can change things up whenever and however he wants.

● ● ●

If your girlfriend asks your life plans, don't say that you're probably going to get a drink later that night. You may not have a girlfriend very much longer.

Remember: In writing, running, and life, often the HARDEST thing to do is getting started. Taking the first step is 90% of the battle.

* * *

Learn the wisdom of staying quiet; the poised beauty of simply walking away. Just because the other person is acting like a jerk, doesn't mean you have to.

* * *

Get proficient at writing and speaking. At some point in time, you're going to have to sell yourself – whether in a job, a relationship, or to get yourself out of trouble.

And if you're speaking, one page on
Microsoft word equals around four minutes.
Also remember, no speech should be more
than eight! It's commercial time after that.

* * *

Don't be self-conscious when you dance.
Dancing is nothing more than giving in to the
power music has over you. Just go with it.

* * *

Get to know your teachers and/or bosses –
they can be cool people, too.

Never take the prescription drug Lomotil unless you don't want to go to the bathroom for a month. Or more.

● ● ●

Call your mom. If you only KNEW how much that will make her day!

● ● ●

Remember, just because you "said it to their face" doesn't make it any better. Being mean is being mean…period!

Keep your room, work and life space neat.
Clear your clutter, clear your mind!

* * *

Also, keep your trunk clean. It's a good
feeling, plus you won't have to move crap all
over the place when you have a flat tire.

* * *

Never wear clothes that are too small for you.
It makes you look fat.

* * *

Have cliques, but don't be afraid to socialize
outside of them. Outside opinions can
sometimes make a big difference.

Remember the three rules about money: Save when you can, be generous when you can, and if you owe it, pay it!

❀ ❀ ❀

Your body, your rules!

❀ ❀ ❀

My quote: "If you don't play your cards, God will shuffle your deck."

❀ ❀ ❀

Learn to shut up and simply listen. You'll be AMAZED at how often people will thank you for your "advice," even though you never said anything. People just want to be heard.

Never play intramural basketball with hernia. Fouling out will be the least of your problems.

● ● ●

Every now and then, put on some classical music. Stuff you normally listen to can make you think too much.

● ● ●

Don't travel with people unless you like them a lot. If you're single, often going alone is a good option.

● ● ●

Force nothing! Be yourself and the right people, places, and conditions will find you.

Or said this way, 'if you lead with love, all else will follow.'

* * *

Invest in shaving cream. If you're going to rip your skin open, at least it makes you feel better.

* * *

Remember this Universal law: When two drunks start wrestling, they will ALWAYS end up fighting.

Something I learned:
Never throw a snowball at your brother when
he's trying to use the bathroom.
He'll be embarrassed… and pretty mad.

● ● ●

Compliment people on their shoes, whether
you really like them or not. It leads to some
really interesting conversations.

● ● ●

Be the kind of person you'd like to
hang out with. After all, wherever you go,
there you'll be.

When in doubt, never forget that there's NEVER anything wrong with being nice.

* * *

Make haste slowly. The people who are supposed to be in your life will be.

* * *

Every night that starts with Jägermeister won't end well – and you won't remember it even if it does.

* * *

If you're the smartest kid in the room, then you're in the wrong room.

When someone raises their voice, lower yours. It'll be the only way to be heard.

* * *

If on a date, open her car door and walk her to her apartment door. There are some advantages of being old school.

* * *

Never play flag football wearing loafers. Your feet will HATE you – for at least 6 days.

* * *

Uber and cab drivers are out there. Make use of them!

Take time every day for yourself and for yourself alone. Once you get past your own insanity, it ends up being a great way to actually stay sane.

● ● ●

When out socially, put your cell phone away. It's amazing how with all these communication gadgets, we've become such horrible communicators!

● ● ●

If you are the designated driver, put the drunk in the front seat. Getting thrown up on the back of your head is simply NOT fun.

Don't be depressed if you don't have your whole life figured out. I had no clue until I was 30 – sometimes I still wonder when I'm freezing my butt off at carpool.

● ● ●

Remember the Dalai Lama's quote: "Be kind whenever possible. It is always possible."

● ● ●

Take time for travel, but make sure there's gas in your car first. Getting pulled by a tow truck doesn't make for a very good vacation.

Don't worry if the handshake has gone by way of the dinosaur. A polite bow will do. Besides, you don't know where those hands have been anyway.

● ● ●

Remember my quote: "Comfort zones are for people who don't have the guts to keep growing."

● ● ●

Call her. Call him. If you're not nervous about it, you're not dreaming big enough.

If you're involved in something and you're loving it so much you lose track of time, THAT is what you want to do for a living! Also, think of what you'd do for free.

● ● ●

Be wary of what's in punch bowls – the contents in those things could either cure or start cancer.

● ● ●

Work on your weaknesses, but also get better at your strengths. Again, your strengths are where you're going to make your living.

Be inclusive. Some of us still haven't gotten over constantly getting picked last for kickball in high school gym class.

● ● ●

Never pretend to be asleep in your room when your friends are up late talking. You might hear something you don't want to hear. Trust me on that one.

● ● ●

Losing my man card, but a quote from "Fried Green Tomatoes": "A heart may break but it keeps beating just the same."

Never strike a match near gas. I mean, seriously, who does that?

● ● ●

When you walk her to the door, hold her head before you try to kiss her. Having her turn sideways and kissing her on the ear can be and was terribly embarrassing…

● ● ●

Don't get in the habit of skipping class. Why make things harder than they already are?

When someone frustrates you and you can't
get through to them, get calm,
THEN send them an email. This way,
they can NOT interrupt you and they
HAVE to see your point.

● ● ●

When you're in a relationship and your other
tells you to 'sit down, we need to talk', when
you stand back up, you probably won't be in
a relationship anymore.

● ● ●

Remember, you'll get over your ex, but you
may never get over your dog.

Don't believe people when they say it's "location, location, location." It's actually location, chemistry, and timing – with all three equally as important.

● ● ●

Remember the three rules of public speaking: Be brief, be brilliant, be gone!

● ● ●

Every so often and for no particular reason, pick up a ball and glove and go play catch. It takes you back and in a good way.

● ● ●

Learn to like apples. I read somewhere that they can wake you up better than coffee.

You can often tell a person's character
by the way they treat a waiter.

● ● ●

If you have to edit yourself too much in a job
interview or a relationship, you're probably
going for the wrong job or in the wrong
relationship.

● ● ●

If you coach, build your system around your
talent; don't try to make your talent fit into
your system.

● ● ●

Yes, absence really does make the heart grow
fonder – of someone else!

Be thankful to whoever invented Raid.
Nothing kills a roach faster –
not even your foot.

● ● ●

If you ever sing the National Anthem, don't
over-sing it like most do. The words are
powerful enough; there's no law that says the
last note has to be 10-plus seconds long.

● ● ●

Always remember, there's nothing better
than a good teacher or coach. Conversely,
there's not much worse than a bad one.

Don't worry if you can't tell the difference between a good rapper or a bad one. After all these years, I'm not real sure there's a difference.

● ● ●

In all due respect to bungee jumping, skydiving, and the like, stick to sports where it won't kill you if you something goes wrong.

● ● ●

Play golf with your dad…and don't even bother to keep score.

Remember, if you cheat society, somewhere down the road society will cheat you back.

● ● ●

After saying "I do" at the altar, never turn to a friend and ask the score of a college football game. It won't get the marriage off to a very good start.

● ● ●

And while I'm at it, don't turn on ESPN when you get back to the Honeymoon Suite either.

When somebody won't pay back what they
owe you, stay positive!
The money will come back in a different way
and from a different source.

* * *

Don't watch the news before going to bed,
and don't sleep with the TV on. Be careful
what goes into your mind, particularly when
you're not awake enough to guard it.

* * *

Learn how to say no. Be polite but remember
you don't have to explain. Smile brightly
while blowing them off.

If someone tries to cut in when you're slow dancing with a hot girl, if the guy is smaller than you, simply say no. After all, you're the one who asked her to dance, right?

● ● ●

Be the designated driver sometimes. Night life can be interesting with a clear perspective.

● ● ●

Always use fighting as a last resort, but if you have to do it, don't worry about fighting fair. After all, if things were fair you wouldn't be fighting in the first place.

Win, lose, and tie with class, and don't forget to learn from all three scenarios.

❋ ❋ ❋

Never run up a score on an opponent. We may not keep perfect records, but karma always does.

❋ ❋ ❋

Learn the names of the people who keep your school or office clean and call them by it.

❋ ❋ ❋

Have access to a punching bag. There WILL be days when you WILL need it.

If you're in a relationship, do NOT forget Valentine's Day for crying out loud! Because that's exactly what she'll do – cry out loud. Good luck to you after that.

● ● ●

Take responsibility for your words and your actions. You will find that MANY of your problems are your very own fault.

● ● ●

If you see a penny on the ground, pick it up whether it's on heads or tails. It's still worth something, right?

Get in a habit of reading if you can. Almost every successful human I've ever heard of is or was an avid reader.

● ● ●

Keep it simple. And remember, if you can use common sense you won't have to think.

● ● ●

Remember Oscar Wilde's quote: Be yourself. Everyone else is taken.

● ● ●

Some good advice from my first boss: Get to work on time or your ass is fired!

Disregard books that tell you to begin by meditating 20 minutes a day. Start with one minute. Twenty minutes is like teaching a beginner the topspin lob on the first lesson.

● ● ●

EVERYONE has a sob story. The question is, what are you going to be about yours – complain or make it a gain?
Your life, your choice.

● ● ●

Focus on solutions, not problems! Unless you're trying to figure out a math problem. Then just go do something else.

Unless you have kids, use your 20s as trial and error. Win. Lose. Laugh. Cry. Throw things. When you hit 30, you should know. If not, there's always grad school.

● ● ●

When people tell you they'll call you sometime, they probably won't. When she says, it's not you, it's me, it's pretty much you.

● ● ●

Don't play with fire. Then again, why would you do that?

● ● ●

Trust your gut. That's where God lives.

If you can't decide, flip a coin. When it's in the air, you'll know which choice you prefer.

● ● ●

Tell your story, even if you have to be a bit vulnerable. Vulnerability is where the growth lies anyway, so let he or she who is sinless cast the first stone.

● ● ●

Never swing off a vine into water unless there's actually water under there. I'm sharing this one for a friend.

Write down your goals but put them down in pencil. Sometimes God needs to borrow the eraser.

❀ ❀ ❀

When your mind starts going down the crapper, sit for a minute or two and do nothing but take long, slow, deep breaths.

❀ ❀ ❀

When having a 50-50 choice about which job to take, take half the day as if you've taken one, then use the other half as if you've taken the other. When did you feel better?

When someone tells you that they have a stomach virus, NEVER ask for details.

● ● ●

You will lose some, but NEVER lose because of overconfidence. That's something you can control, therefore there is no excuse for it.

● ● ●

Never celebrate after a good play. Act like you do it all the time.

● ● ●

Remember this:
"That space between humility and quiet confidence – that is the space from where you should live and compete."

And this: "Be yourself – the world will adjust." That's a tad mind-blowing, but I'm weird enough to like it.

● ● ●

End one relationship before you start another. After all, dating one person is hard enough.

● ● ●

Disrespect NO ONE!

● ● ●

If you're driving the bus and you've set a departure time, leave at that time. Someone will get left – once – but they'll never be late again.

Always know that it IS legal to turn left on yellow. Either learn that or take up a new life for yourself at the corner of Roswell Road and Hammond Drive.

* * *

Be likeable. That way, if you're ever in a 50-50 situation, the odds will swing in your favor most if not all the time. This is underrated, but important.

* * *

Do your job and then some.

In doubles in tennis, always poach on the first point. You may get passed, but your opponent will likely miss the next few returns worrying about you.

● ● ●

But you may want to reconsider that if your partner's serve blows. Getting hit in the head with an optic yellow tennis ball is no good way to start your day.

● ● ●

When in a group, always notice who people look at when they laugh at something. That's the person they're the most into.

Don't wait until New Year's Eve to make resolutions. If something needs adding, changing, or fixing, do it now. Who knows when your last day will be anyway?

* * *

If someone is talking to you and their feet aren't pointing towards you, they likely don't want to be talking to you in the first place.

* * *

About once every three months, check into a hotel room alone with your computer, a good book, and the drink of your choice. It's your night, your time, your recharging.

And to pay for it, put about $30 on a credit card per each paycheck in advance. That way, the night will be already paid for upon checkout.

● ● ●

And throw away the receipt. Your significant other may not understand or, at the least, might find you a bit odd.

● ● ●

Now and again, strike up a conversation with a stranger. People's stories are fascinating, mind-enhancing, often inspiring. Besides, you already know your friend's stories.

Remember and appreciate this Brene Brown quote: "Life is in the ordinary. We often miss it by looking for the extraordinary."

● ● ●

Write sober, edit buzzed. When you're buzzed, your attention span becomes as short as your audience's will be. This will make omitting extra words easy to do.

● ● ●

Remember this Martin Luther King quote and try to live by it: "You don't have to see the whole staircase, just take the first step!"

Or put another way – a sign on the Library of Congress reads: "When a web is begun, God sends thread."

* * *

Cultivate gratitude. When you focus on what you're thankful for, the Man upstairs sends you more to be thankful for.

* * *

Trust waiters when they tell you the plate is hot.

* * *

Take naps. When you wake up in your own drool, you're good to go.

Give your significant other a
massage every now and then.

＊ ＊ ＊

Get a sports massage every now and then.
A tight body equals a tight mind.

＊ ＊ ＊

Please note: The ONLY thing that
goes good with tequila is a pillow.

＊ ＊ ＊

To avoid trouble, just say "I hear you,"
when talking to a drunk. They'll think you're
agreeing with them even if you're not.

When taking a new job or going someplace new, instead of announcing your presence with authority, first learn what the presence of the place IS. Then take it from there.

● ● ●

Try not to sleep in the same room with your cell phone. Set your daily goals first without letting social media and/or emails set the tone for your day.

● ● ●

And end your day by writing down at least three good things that happened. Falling asleep to the positives will pay dividends when waking in the morning.

If you get nostalgic for your high school days,
read "Be True to Your School"
by Bob Greene.

● ● ●

When teaching, use the "crap sandwich"
method: start with a positive, put the problem
in the middle; then end with a positive.
They'll leave wanting to help you.

● ● ●

Remember this: Life is a mirror –
you get back what you put out.

● ● ●

Drink water instead of gin. No matter what
the commercials say, water is better for you.

Go snorkeling or learn how to scuba dive.
It's very peaceful.

* * *

Congratulations if you don't like booze! This
will save SO much time and SO much money!

* * *

At least once, make yourself speak in public.
You'll pee in your pants in nervousness, but it
will build confidence. Or, if nothing else, it
will be something to laugh about later.

* * *

Remember this quote from a coach regarding
overconfidence: "Don't take off your jock
until there's no time on the clock!"

Don't forget to laugh.

● ● ●

Remember: There's no such thing as a good seat for a meeting. And make sure you have a good exit strategy regardless of where you end up.

● ● ●

NEVER take part in men vs. women arguments. Instead, quietly know it takes both kinds to make a world.

● ● ●

Never forget brainless fun such as board games, water slides, and putt putt.

Never trust a man who says trust me.

● ● ●

And another 'never': If you happen to get divorced, NEVER make a major decision until at least six months later. You'll end up having to re-do everything you just did.

● ● ●

Don't shoot yourself in the finger with a gun. I actually know somebody who did that. Still not sure why.

● ● ●

Forgive yourself. This one's hard sometimes but remind yourself you're doing the best you can with what you know at the time.

When you're having a bad day,
make someone else smile. Congrats!
Your day just got better.

⬤ ⬤ ⬤

Use your time in the shower for gratitude.
After all, 85% of the people on the planet don't
have the luxury of a shower to begin with.

⬤ ⬤ ⬤

Never stop learning! I mean, we thought we
had it all figured out, then we suffered
through the coronavirus and an election in
the same year!

⬤ ⬤ ⬤

Buy a veteran a cup of coffee.

When telling a story, get to the point! Life is short, plus, other people want to talk, too.

● ● ●

Remember Morgan Freeman's quote: Never take criticism from someone you wouldn't take advice from.

● ● ●

If you want your mind blown, read "Conversations with God, Book 1" by Neale Donald Walsch.

● ● ●

When you hug someone, hug them like you mean it! But remember to let her go if she starts to get uncomfortable.

If you start a business, do NOT charge hidden fees! This will make you perhaps unusual in this country, but priceless as well.

. . .

Stop using the "f' word! You may think it's cool when you're younger, but as you age, not so much.

. . .

Leave 'em laughing. But try to forget the time you tried being a comedian and no one even giggled.

If you're a softball pitcher and someone hits a line drive back up the box, for God's sakes duck! Your head, your doctor's bill, and your health will all thank you.

● ● ●

Don't be late – it's rude! In fact, be early when you can.

● ● ●

Don't apologize for succeeding. Just say thanks for the compliment and keep on kicking butt.

● ● ●

Remember: the more people involved in a committee, the dumber the final decision.

Ask yourself this: Do I own my possessions, or do they own me? If it's the ladder, then make the adjustments.

* * *

In a world demanding you look to the future, work instead on staying in the present. After all, the future is promised to no one.

* * *

If you're in bed and the room is spinning, get up and throw up first; then go back to bed.

* * *

Respect the Bible but write your own and live it for a year. Then repeat the process.

Remember: You make your own luck by preparation, positivity, and productivity.

● ● ●

And remember the seven P's: Proper planning and preparation prevents piss poor performance.

● ● ●

If you read an article you like, send a note telling the writer. After all, writing can be a lonely profession and they usually don't hear anything except criticisms.

● ● ●

It's usually not what you say, but how you say it.

Don't always root for the underdogs. After all, sometimes they are underdogs for a reason.

● ● ●

Don't be so quick to hand someone your business card. Connect at a deeper level if you can. Also, odds are they'll just throw it away anyway.

● ● ●

Quit trying to change others and work on changing yourself.

● ● ●

Remember this saying: Of course I'm cracked, that's how the light gets in!

If you need to take a nap, turn on a golf tournament. Those announcer's voices will put you to sleep every time.

● ● ●

Be nice to people who work carpool. After all, that job can suck!

● ● ●

If you get dumped, it's perfectly okay to admit it. These things happen.

● ● ●

Know when to keep your goals to yourself. People can be negative and shoot down your great ideas.

Quit complaining. After all, this is the day
God has made – go ye forth and rejoice in it.

● ● ●

As you get older, become an early riser.
That's when God's voice is most clear.

● ● ●

Every hour of sleep you get before midnight
is worth two after.

● ● ●

Stay up all night at least once –
just to say you did it.

Never take more money to the poker table than you're prepared to lose.

● ● ●

Remember: Just because someone will have a drink with you doesn't necessarily make them a friend. Friendship is a marathon, not a sprint.

● ● ●

Two underrated things: The plank when stretching and Spirulina when taking supplements.

For back troubles, lay on a hard wood floor for 20 minutes a day. It's not as uncomfortable as it sounds.

● ● ●

Always wait before congratulating a distance runner after a great race or workout. Getting puked on is no fun.

● ● ●

Speaking of, never puke in your roommate's car. It's not good for the relationship.

● ● ●

Let other people dominate the conversations. You never learn anything when you're talking anyway.

If you're going to take off your helmet after a good play, then take it off after a bad one. Fair is fair.

● ● ●

Before an athletic event, avoid trash talking. After all, why make the opponent more fired up to beat you than he already is?

● ● ●

And after the game, do the fist bump instead of the handshake. The law of average says, at least one of the people you're shaking hands with is sick.

If someone pulls your shorts down while you're holding your dining hall tray, do your best to forgive them.

* * *

Never burp in your date's ear. Most of them don't like that very much.

* * *

Put your phone out of reach when you're driving. Whatever it is, it's not worth dying over.

* * *

Never get so self-important that you can't dress up for Halloween.

If you're not into the weight room,
at least do some pushups every day.

● ● ●

Send a Christmas card to someone you barely
know. It's worth it just to see the shocked
look on their face the next time they see you.

● ● ●

Make sure your shorts are secured before
going on a water slide. Otherwise, the
ensuing pictures will not make your mom
proud.

● ● ●

Treat someone to a Smoothie.

Be careful of posing for pictures when at a party. Future employers are known to check social media when deciding whether or not to hire you.

● ● ●

Be creative when buying Christmas gifts. Get personal in a good way.

● ● ●

Keep a pen in your pocket, and if something resonates with you, write it down. Still, good luck if the pen busts – the stain will NOT come out.

When going on the first date, dress the same way you did when you were wooing her in the first place.

● ● ●

And when on an interview, dress the way you'd dress if you had the job.

● ● ●

And when interviewing, NEVER complain about your last job! If you complain about that, they figure you'll complain about the job you're trying to get.

Beds are fine, but every now and then, there's not a much freer feeling than sleeping on your couch.

● ● ●

Talk to your plants.
They know if you care or not.

● ● ●

Don't talk to your shoes, though.
People may think you're weird.

● ● ●

If you must go out and paint the town red or beige or anywhere in between, coat your stomach first.

Keep your emails short and,
if it is a little long, skip a space between each
paragraph. Makes it less daunting and more
likely to get read.

● ● ●

In writing, conversations, dates, bonding,
and life its own self, always try to end on a
good note.

● ● ●

Quit when you're ahead. Unless you're
playing poker and you have all the money,
then that could be a little tough to do.

Compliment women when they're dressed nice but also let them know they look just as good when dressed normally.

● ● ●

Hang up pictures in your room that make you smile. Nothing negative allowed.

● ● ●

Every now and then, clean out the numbers in your cell phone. If you haven't called or thought about them in years, you're probably not going to start now.

If you're going to publicly disagree with someone on social media, make sure you compliment them on something every now and then as well.

● ● ●

Every now and then, play charades and/or go swing in the park.

● ● ●

Go watch little kids play a soccer game. Seeing 22 little ones chase one ball around is hilarious.

● ● ●

Don't take too long in the shower. We may need the water one day.

Argue for what you're for, not what you're against. What you focus on expands.

* * *

If you walk in on your roommate at a bad time, never tell him exactly what you saw.

* * *

Trust in God but lock your car.

* * *

When playing chess,
don't underestimate the pawn.

If you end up substitute teaching, bulk up on your Vitamin C and supplements. After all, you're always going to be sitting at a sick person's desk.

* * *

Speaking of, get in a good habit of washing your hands. A lot.

* * *

"Self-important people are preposterous. We come, we do, we go, and we shouldn't take ourselves any more seriously than that." – Robert James Waller

* * *

Attend an outdoor concert. Tailgate.

But make sure you have the tickets. Dates really do NOT like it when you don't.

. . .

Compose an essay, poem, or music from the heart. Afterwards, no matter how nervous, hit the 'submit' button.

. . .

Visit New England. In the summer.

. . .

Jog on a golf course.

If a snake is coiled up around your golf ball when you find it in the woods, just take the two-stroke penalty and move on.

● ● ●

Never take the top off the blender when it's in use. Mom will get REALLY mad.

● ● ●

Don't throw away your clip-on tie. Your friends will laugh VERY hard at you, but you may need to save the time someday.

Have a general plan, but rarely a specific one. Leave room for adlibs and trips off the beaten path, as that's usually where the most fun happens anyway.

● ● ●

When setting up an appointment, figure when you can get there, then add 30 minutes. It's never fun to be in a hurry if something comes up.

● ● ●

Never leave a mess. The Universe likes order.

If you have a younger brother who
borrows your car and ends up driving
it into a ditch, go easy on him.
He just wanted to go on a joy ride.

● ● ●

Forgive but don't forget.

● ● ●

In this era of debit and credit cards, keep
some cash in your pocket. Supporting
lemonade stands and the like can be
rewarding for all involved.

And as far as money, try to adopt Shakespeare's philosophy: "Neither a borrower nor a lender be."

∘ ∘ ∘

Find a charity you believe in and donate to it from time to time.

∘ ∘ ∘

If your favorite coffee shop is out of French vanilla, remember hazelnut works just about as well.

∘ ∘ ∘

In the work world, be proactive in creating the job you want. You'll be surprised how fast rejections can turn into green lights later.

Never applaud when you find out your older brother totaled your junk of a car. It's more polite to ask how he is first. Reporting this one for a friend.

* * *

Never go to your Homecoming with one date and then come home with another. Neither the parents nor the dates will understand.

* * *

Believe in miracles. Ghosts are optional.

* * *

Don't run a marathon until you're at least 20 years old. Your legs need to fully develop first.

And speaking of running: Always know there
is NOTHING more gross than a porta-john
before a marathon or big race.

* * *

Don't pee in the shower.

* * *

Never go straight to bed after a long day.
Take some time to veg out first –
get tired slowly.

* * *

And if you're sick, sleep and water are great
cures for just about everything.

Handwrite a note to a relative who has passed on. I'm weird enough to believe they can and will read it.

● ● ●

If you want to be left alone at work, just grab a notepad, walk down the halls, and talk to yourself. No one will come near you, I promise.

● ● ●

If your boss calls you in for a meeting, bring the notepad with you. You may need it.

Be careful when body surfing among huge waves. Those things can hurt you!

● ● ●

As far as body weight, maintain a certain pants size and NEVER waver on this. If things get tight, eat less and exercise more.

● ● ●

And if the pants get too tight, it's NOT because they've been washed a lot. It's because the food has been good.

● ● ●

If you have a cholesterol problem, fall in love with oatmeal.

When you write a sweet note to your significant other, always hand write it, don't put it on a computer. Handwriting is more personal – from the head to the hand to the heart.

* * *

Don't go to bed mad. Do some deep breathing, punch your pillow, or scream at the TV – whatever works. But don't take it out on your dog.

* * *

Have a side hustle.

* * *

Frequent mom and pop bookstores – assuming there are any left.

Never have too many drinks at the company Christmas party. Drunk comments are sober thoughts, and it seems bosses are trained to know this.

❋ ❋ ❋

If it's cold, don't complain - just put on layers. Why people gripe about the weather while warm clothes hang at home in their closets is beyond me.

❋ ❋ ❋

Go for runs in the rain, but never during thunder and lightning.

Every now and then,
let a dog lick you in the face.

● ● ●

Find an object that's sacred to you for your
reasons only. Don't even explain, just have it
handy, just because.

● ● ●

Try to forgive your college friend if he threw
up on your couch and tried to hide it under
the cushion.

● ● ●

When you get a text, respond to it – even if
it's just to let them know you got it.

When you're incredibly ticked off at someone, write them the nastiest note ever! Then throw it away, sleep on it, and rethink things tomorrow.

* * *

Whether you're into it or not, try to meditate at least once. It's not easy, but beneficial.

* * *

When you're changing your tire, don't take off the whole wheel. This doesn't work out very well.

* * *

Respect the art of teaching. And try it sometime.

Volunteer to give the sermon at your church at least once in your life. It will scare the hell out of you – literally – but it also could prove life changing.

● ● ●

Learn one of your classmates' sports stats. You'll be more than amazed at how much that will impress them.

● ● ●

For that matter, learn fun facts about as many people as you can. If nothing else, it leads to great conversations.

If you drink your mom's champagne, never re-cork the bottle and put it back in the refrigerator. I promise you, she's not that dumb.

● ● ●

If you're on the school's cross country team and you sometimes run off and sit in the woods, guess what? There's a great chance your coaches DO know about it.

● ● ●

If you meet a celebrity, ask about their kids, do NOT talk about the celebrity. You'll be amazed at the neat conversations you can have.

Speaking of, notice the facial expression of a mother when you're talking about her kid. There's nothing quite so peaceful or beautiful.

● ● ●

If you're a guy, never ever wear a girls' pair of overalls into a college history class. You will never live it down.

● ● ●

Every now and then,
binge watch a series on Netflix.

Don't always buy the cheapest item. Instead, let your subconscious know that you are worth, and can afford, more than that.

*   *   *

Always ask before putting more salt on the chips when in a Mexican restaurant.

*   *   *

And remember:
Chips and salsa are NOT major food groups.

*   *   *

If you get pulled over, always make a show out of trying to find your license. It lets the cop know immediately that you don't have to pull it out very much.

And if you've lived and/or worked at the same place for a long time, casually "slip" that into the conversation as well. It lets them know you're a stable human being.

● ● ●

Invest some of your money. Otherwise you're actually losing it due to inflation.

● ● ●

If you're single, try living alone for a while if you can afford it. No one has to know that nobody wanted to room with you.

Get rid of any jealousies you may have. Instead, spend the same amount of time and energy developing your own self. Let other people start envying you.

● ● ●

Never get mad if you don't get the athletic uniform of your favorite player. Get your own number; start your own thing. One day, someone may want your number.

● ● ●

If possible, try to take some time in your day to simply goof off. Ironically, that's often when the best ideas come.

When changing locations,
strongly consider hiring movers.
Some things are worth paying for. Same with
taxes unless you're wired that way.

❂ ❂ ❂

If you're single, remember her phone
number. That way, when you recite it back to
her, she'll believe it when you say you've
been meaning to call.

❂ ❂ ❂

Get a box and keep your random stuff in it –
concert tickets, pictures, movie stubs, report
cards, vacations. This will become priceless
over time.

Don't smoke. That sometimes leads to drugs which leads to….

* * *

Every now and then, schedule an appointment with a holistic doctor.

* * *

Get in a good habit of stretching – daily if possible.

* * *

Don't throw a bottle at a sign while in the passenger seat of a car. If could bounce back and hit you. (Or so I'm told…)

Never underestimate the good feeling of making a pretty woman laugh.

● ● ●

But don't get carried away with that if she's sitting next to her boyfriend.

● ● ●

Every once in a while, soak in a hot tub.

● ● ●

And rent a cabin for a weekend in the mountains.

Cherish long, innocent conversations and avoid people with hidden agendas. Approach people needing nothing; if something is meant to be yours, it will find you.

● ● ●

Buy and own a favorite coffee mug.

● ● ●

Whether you like professional baseball or not, go to a game at Wrigley Field and/or Fenway Park.

If you hit it big in the slots in Vegas, put some of the winnings in your pocket. Otherwise, you'll keep putting the coins back in until you lose it all.

⚙ ⚙ ⚙

If you get a bad feeling in your gut about something or someone, it's usually for a reason. Pay attention!

⚙ ⚙ ⚙

Don't pull your sister's hair. That's mean!

⚙ ⚙ ⚙

Never jump on a moving train. It's very adventurous, but also very dangerous.

Take the job that's your passion, even if it pays less than the one you have now. You'll make the money back within a year because you'll be among like-minded people.

● ● ●

Remember the 8/8/8 rule. If you like your eight hours at work, you'll like your eight hours when you're off, and as a result, you'll sleep well in the other eight.

● ● ●

And when you're interviewing, don't even wait for the questions. Just fire away with what you can do for them and how your talents match. Impress them!

Never walk in with your tie out of your collar, pepperoni pizza on your shirt, and/or mustard on your shoes. That's probably not their dress code.

● ● ●

Change up your routine sometimes. Don't let your brain get hardwired due to doing the exact same things. Leave room for adventure/exploration; keep the brain young!

● ● ●

Be careful when diving into a lake. If there's a board just below the surface, this can REALLY hurt. Unfortunately, I'm speaking from experience.

If you go skinny dipping, remember where you put your clothes. Not knowing this can prove terribly embarrassing.

● ● ●

If you're jogging or working carpool, don't always assume the cars will stop for you.

● ● ●

Never kill an animal just for the "sport" of it. Unless it's a roach.

● ● ●

Give blood every now and then. It's the equivalent to changing the oil in your car.

Don't scrimp on going to the doctor. Why people take better care of their cars than they do their bodies is way beyond me.

● ● ●

If you have to get a biopsy for prostate cancer, find a doctor that will put you to sleep.

● ● ●

Find a dentist that gives free goofy gas.

● ● ●

On special days, buy her something more creative than just flowers.

Don't wait until the angry Doberman is
chasing you to pray. Pray often.

● ● ●

It's been written that "once you learn to love
yourself, then everything you want will come
to you." Sounds good to me, though
sometimes tough to do.

● ● ●

Be careful of doing tai chi with a mirror in
front of you. After all, the instructor is liable
to get really ticked off when you start
laughing at yourself. Same with aerobics.

Respect karate as much or more for the discipline than the fighting part of it.

● ● ●

Never let a passenger in your car flip off a motorcycle gang. The aftermath will NOT be pretty.

● ● ●

Be very careful when scaling a barbed wire fence. Otherwise, you might climb up as a man and come down a woman.

When your mind goes into the crapper, simply repeat "Thank you, I love you," over and over again in your head. It'll be a big improvement, not to mention a good prayer.

● ● ●

When you have a cold, keep sticking your face in bowls of chicken noodle soup.

● ● ●

Whatever your workout regiment, take at least one day off a week. Sometimes rest equals training!

If you do go through a divorce, take your share of the responsibility for it. And don't become one of those bitter "hate the opposite" sex types. No one wants to hear it.

● ● ●

Find an inspirational book, movie, or video and start your day with it. It sets a much better tone than hitting the snooze button the allotted seven times.

● ● ●

Travel. It undoes a lot of your brains habitual wiring – and in a good way.

If you find yourself lip syncing when you're in the choir, you probably shouldn't be in the choir to begin with.

* * *

Support your local musicians, artists, and authors and learn their stories.

* * *

Don't rehearse an upcoming big conversation. Let it flow and be natural.

* * *

Speaking of, know when to go with the flow and know when to create it.

Remember this: Too much "me" ruins the team, and too much team ruins the "me." Learn when to blend and when to step up.

● ● ●

It's not confusing – life is what you make of it, so make it a good one. After all, you are the author.

● ● ●

Never tell your sister that she's fat. It's not good for family relations or dinner table conversations.

Every now and then, call a friend you haven't spoken to in a while. If nothing else, it'll break up the monotony, maybe set you on a different course.

● ● ●

Learn CPR. I saw it save a life once.

● ● ●

Be loyal to your favorite teams – whether high school, college, or pro. People that switch to whoever happens to be winning are nauseating.

If someone tells you the clothes you're wearing are old, simply smile. After all, at least you can still fit in them.

● ● ●

While it may be true that 'what happens in Vegas, stays in Vegas,' in this day and time, what you do may wind up on social media. Be careful!

● ● ●

If possible, keep or make peace with your parents. They have done, are doing, and will do the best they can knowing what they know. And I'm sure they mean well.

Never watch "The Amityville Horror" and then try to go to sleep. It's not a good combination.

* * *

And no matter what you did that night, never sleep in your closet. You have a bed, right?

* * *

You don't have to solve the world's problems in one day, but you can do some positive, little things every day.

* * *

Don't exaggerate.

Remember this Zig Ziglar quote:
"If you don't think this is a good day,
then try missing one of them."

● ● ●

Brush your teeth. Otherwise, you're going to
be one disgusting individual.

● ● ●

If a Peaches and Herb song comes on the
radio, don't sing along. You might lose your
man card. (I got rejected while "Reunited"
was playing; bad attitude on my part!)

Appreciate it when a group of people do 'The Electric Slide' or any group dance like that. Seeing choreography in motion can be rather refreshing.

● ● ●

Take out the trash. The flies won't appreciate it, but you and/or your roommates will.

● ● ●

When you go out, leave your TV on. It's one of THE best ways to keep from getting burglarized.

But when your girlfriend wants to talk, it's best to turn it off. Laughing at a 'That 70s Show' episode during a 'key moment' may not be best for the relationship.

● ● ●

Clean up after your dog when outside.

● ● ●

But when he swallows your pen, wait until he 'runs out of ink' before doing one mass cleaning.

If you have chiggers, scratch them until they bleed, then put rubbing alcohol on them. Not great for the skin, but more effective than clear fingernail polish.

● ● ●

Then again, rubbing alcohol is an underrated cure for a lot of things – zits included.

● ● ●

NEVER show up your opponent in anything. Remember, what goes around comes around.

If you're sore, buy some Epsom Salts
and draw a hot bath -
but try not to fall asleep in the tub.

● ● ●

After a marathon, please know that just
because you're not sore a few days later, does
NOT mean you've recovered! Coming back
too soon equals sickness and injury!

● ● ●

And if you want a good laugh, watch people
dance the night after their marathon. They
look like robots that need oiling.

To borrow author Alan Cohen's philosophy:
"If it's not fun, hire it done!"

● ● ●

Be wary of phone scams – people pretending
to be from the IRS or Social Security in
particular. If you have to use 'colorful'
language in brushing them off, so be it.

● ● ●

If you're a coach, never take your MVP for
granted when it comes to handed out awards.
Talk him and her up just as much as the
"Most Improved."

On the same subject,
NEVER forget the athletic director's kid
when giving out the certificates.
Not good for job security I'm told…

● ● ●

Be wary of a stranger that opens with a joke
at your watering hole. They're probably
softening you up to sell you something.

● ● ●

When you're being checked for a hernia at
your physical…good luck. I don't have any
good advice for this whatsoever.

Just know in advance, that a trip
to the doctor is "The Death of Dignity,"
and take it from there.

● ● ●

Do not get into credit card debt – it's hard to
blame that on anyone but yourself.

● ● ●

Simple philosophies on money and weight
maintenance: Make more than you spend and
give out more calories than you take in.
Everything else is just smoke and mirrors.

"Do unto others as you would have them do unto you." Greatest. Rule. Ever.

● ● ●

In the rest room, it really doesn't matter if you leave the seat up or down, just clean up before you leave!

● ● ●

The first phone conversation with your ex will always be the most awkward. There's that silence before hanging up when you used to say, 'I love you.'

Writing and public speaking are actually not hard. All you have to do is cut open your soul and lay it out there for all to see. Let he who is sinless cast the first stone.

● ● ●

If you're not nervous the first time you go rappelling, then maybe you shouldn't be rappelling. It's the nerves that makes you careful – and this is a good thing.

● ● ●

If you can't find a pickup basketball game, practice your free throws. It's great mental practice as well as physical.

Never get in a sauna when you
feel a cold coming on.

● ● ●

And make sure if you do get in one, you
know whether it's coed or not. This is not a
good way to meet a strange woman.

● ● ●

Attend a high school or college football game
and simply take in all the energy.

● ● ●

Before openly berating sports announcers, try
it sometime. Unlike writing, there's no
'delete' button once something is said.

Don't miss all the good because you're
focused on all the bad.

* * *

Feed the ducks, whether the snacks
are gluten free or not.

* * *

And never stick your hand inside the lion
cage at the zoo. Why would you do that?

* * *

Every once in a while, and for no particular
reason, walk up and hug your mother. If she
doesn't cry on the outside, I promise she will
be on the inside.

Take good care of your feet. And every now and again, buy some new socks.

● ● ●

If invited, be the 'third wheel' every now and then. It often comes out sort of fun.

● ● ●

Never put oil in the radiator.
It's not good for the car. Duh.

● ● ●

Speaking of, don't scrimp on your car maintenance. You'll either pay some now or a whole lot more later.

Don't take things or people for granted.
Always appreciate your parents, your health,
and, of course, whoever invented
the remote control.

● ● ●

If you want to become a cliff diver, good luck.
Not exactly sure how you train for that.

● ● ●

Do your absolute best to create a life you fall
in love with. After all, love wins.

If you've just done or achieved something awesome, let someone else bring it up in conversation. Do NOT bring it up yourself.

● ● ●

Never fart in an elevator. It's rude.

● ● ●

Keep as many pictures of your high school and college days as you can.
During tough times, looking back over these can lift your spirits.

● ● ●

If you're thinking about having the extra glass of booze, don't.

Take as few pharmaceutical drugs as possible. They cure one problem but create three more.

● ● ●

Hydrate. If you don't, this can and will open Pandora's Box.

● ● ●

Reread your favorite book and/or re-watch your favorite movie.

● ● ●

If the ball's above the rim, slam it home. Don't pull it back, dribble to half court, then try score the hard way just where you'll look smart. Let things be easy if you can.

If you're playing shirts and skins in hoops, never put on somebody else's sweaty shirt. It's a very gross feeling.

● ● ●

Make a cute 20-second video on your phone and send it to one of your friends. Start their day off with a smile.

● ● ●

Don't fall in love with mixed martial arts. Something about fighting in a cage makes it more of a hormone problem than a sport.

Be nice to the people in the food serving line. You'll be amazed at how much you have on your plate when you get to the end.

• • •

In sports and in life, change a losing game – even if it means breaking tradition.

• • •

Talking about the bad keeps the bad alive. Instead, silently bless it, then set about trying to change it.

If you're ever on anti-depressants, never go off them cold turkey. Instead, cut the dosage down gradually over time until you're done with them.

● ● ●

Learn how to imitate your teacher's or bosses' movements and personality quirks. Just make sure they're not around when you're making fun of them.

● ● ●

When the weather's nice, fall in love with sitting on your porch.

Be careful who you take advice from. Make SURE they have your best interests in mind.

* * *

Never give a friend money advice. If he doesn't come out well, you may not either.

* * *

Don't hurry to grow up –
it happens too fast as it is.

* * *

Don't underestimate a high school kid's life. It's not like the movie 'Grease' where they meet a hot blonde on the first day, then dance on top of cars the whole time.

Remember: You can learn something from everybody – people come across your path for reasons, good and bad.

● ● ●

Don't pick your nose when you're driving. People can still see you.

● ● ●

And don't take it personally when someone cuts you off on the freeway. Why get to work mad when the offending driver is still happily driving down the road?

If there's a worm in your apple, don't eat it.
You knew that, right?

● ● ●

Find a hobby or hobbies that are so fun you
feel like you're inhaling God when you're
doing them.

● ● ●

Never forget your first real kiss.

● ● ●

But if you're single,
don't tell about your last one.

At least once in your life, attend or work at a summer camp, and make copies of the letters you sent while there. Makes for classic reading later in life.

● ● ●

Go on a train ride – destination who cares?

● ● ●

Visit Asheville, NC – but don't expect to get a parking place when you go downtown.

● ● ●

If you're a jogger, find a great trail to run. I'm pretty sure that's where God lives.

Avoid going to a regular season NBA game.
I've seen more effort in a
Friday afternoon math class.

● ● ●

Avoid 'academic vs. athletic' arguments.
Both are very educational.

● ● ●

Stretch out in front of a fireplace.
When your feet catch on fire,
you'll know it's time to get up.

● ● ●

Let a former teacher or coach know when
you've passed on their lessons. It makes up
for the pay they don't get. Sort of.

Get your picture made while riding a camel –
but make sure you wash your pants later.

＊ ＊ ＊

Appreciate the art of gardening.
I'm told God lives in those things as well.

＊ ＊ ＊

If you go whitewater rafting, always be
prepared to be thrown out of the boat.

＊ ＊ ＊

Never eat an apple fritter right before a run.
They don't taste so good when
they come back up.

Find a good luck charm and take it with you
wherever you go.

● ● ●

Don't desert the God you believe in during
tough times. It's ironic that we often do that.

● ● ●

Go easy on the pizza guy if he's a little late
with the delivery.

● ● ●

Always appreciate the beauty and comfort of
a hoodie or a long-sleeved T-shirt.

Never perform wrestling moves on the dolls your girlfriend sleeps with. She probably won't like that very much.

● ● ●

When negotiating, let the other guy make the first offer. If the two people negotiating just read this, I'm not real sure how that's going to go.

● ● ●

Learn some type of self-defense. It's a crazy world out there.

Avoid strip clubs at all costs. Basically, it's
internal frustrations inside which lead to
external violence outside.

* * *

See the Grand Canyon if you can. And allow
at least 30 minutes while you simply stand in
awe looking at it all.

* * *

Go see a high school play. You'll be amazed
at the talent.

For that matter, be in a play at some point. You won't forget it, even if you're not into acting.

● ● ●

Don't wait to make a bucket list. After all, when exactly are you going to die?

● ● ●

If you're around a teenager, never make a reference to Columbo. They will have NO clue who you're talking about.

● ● ●

When someone in your car says they know a short cut, think twice before believing them.

At some point, drive a bus filled with high school kids. You'll be amazed at the stuff you'll hear, whether you want to hear it or not.

●　●　●

Same with walking through the stretching lines at an athletic practice.

●　●　●

Have a favorite college football team and root for them until they're planting flowers over you.

And if you are a 'house divided' in that regard, make sure you're out of the house when the two teams are playing each other.

* * *

Remember: Class reunions get better as you get older. The early ones are all about what you're doing for a living; the ladder ones more about just being glad to be alive.

* * *

If somebody approaches that you don't want to talk to, just pull out your cell phone and act like you're on a call.

Learn to play a musical instrument.
And unless you're as bad as I was,
perform for someone.

● ● ●

If you have to put on a graduation robe,
make sure you pee first.

● ● ●

If you're finished in the bank teller line,
GET OUT OF THE WAY while looking for
your keys and filing your papers in your
wallet. People are waiting!

● ● ●

Slower traffic keep right.

Same rules apply on a track.

● ● ●

If you're about to tee off, and all the deer run
out of the woods and into the fairway,
you should probably take up another sport
besides golf.

● ● ●

Every now and then, light a candle. It's kind
of spiritual.

● ● ●

If you ever have to get stitches in your lip,
good luck. I try to be positive,
but this hurts pretty bad.

If you ever hit rock bottom, rest up, wake up,
get psyched up, look up, pray up, then bring
your life back up. You've got this!

● ● ●

And when in doubt, you are stronger and
more resilient than you think. Know this!

● ● ●

Never open a bottle with your teeth.
That's just dumb.

● ● ●

If you ever ride the bumper cars at the
amusement park, run into every car in sight.
It's all about getting your money's worth...

If you see an alligator by a lake,
leave it alone. Last I checked,
they don't make very good pets.

❀ ❀ ❀

Don't swim in the ocean at night.
You're in the shark's home, not yours.

❀ ❀ ❀

If you disobey this, try NOT to hear the music
from 'Jaws' as you're wading in.

❀ ❀ ❀

If you want to give up something, give it up
NOW. If you put it off, it means that deep
down you really don't want to give it up.

If you want to write a book, don't be intimidated. If you write a page a day for a year, that's two books right there, maybe even three.

* * *

If you make a speech, call names from the audience and bring them into it. Talk WITH them, not at them. It keeps them from checking their cell phones, temporarily at least.

* * *

And some say to lead with a joke to make you less nervous. But…if you do that and no one laughs, there's a chance you'll have an unplanned bowel movement.

The first night you fall giddy in love, don't go to sleep. Enjoy the feeling for as long as you can without a break in the action.

* * *

Keep bug spray handy. And band aids.

* * *

No matter how big a neat freak you are, have at least one drawer where you throw all your crap. Batteries, and receipts, and random papers, oh my!

If you're an Atlanta sports fan, try REAL hard to forget the 1996 World Series and that Super Bowl game of a few years ago. Yeah, you know which one I'm talking about.

● ● ●

Unless you're a wine snob, don't buy the expensive stuff. Why pay extra money just to impress people you might not even like?

● ● ●

Keep the same philosophy when tempted to keep up with the Jones. Just who the heck are they anyway? And why do they matter so much?

Never let an old person into your brain. And like Satchel Paige once said, "How old would you be if you didn't know when you were born?" Yeah, don't forget that.

* * *

Remember: There's rarely such a thing as a bad workout. You came. You sweated. You did it. And even if your mind was a crap storm, you just got it out of your system.

* * *

The Tony Robbins quote: "Everybody's biggest problem is they think they shouldn't have any." We do. We all do. Remember that before disrespecting someone.

Remember: Everyone needs an editor – in writing and in life.

* * *

If you ever get to stand on the top rung of the podium, respect it, appreciate it, and enjoy the view.

* * *

And never underestimate the people that are standing below you. They've won in their own ways as well.

* * *

Don't ever give up on someone. There's a positive fire in there somewhere.

Do something every day to get yourself to where and who you want to become.

● ● ●

The GPS doesn't start until you start moving. You're waiting on God, God's waiting on you. Go! Take the first step! After that, follow the bouncing ball.

● ● ●

Never dry off with the same towel you cleaned your bathroom with. It won't get your day started right and you won't smell very good.

Appreciate the simple foods – like spaghetti
and clam chowder.

• • •

Carry Kleenex in your pocket, because
wiping snot on your shirt is kind of gross.

• • •

If you're sick, stay home. Take one for the
team by not spreading it around.

• • •

Never sweat bad hair days –
that's what hats are for.

You will never, ever receive more negative unsolicited advice than when you're about to get married. Agreeing with the advice, however, may not get you off to a good start.

● ● ●

Take the time to learn about some deep breathing exercises. It's a great way to unclog your system of stuck energies – a flushing if you will.

● ● ●

Keep a blank check in your wallet and a good book to read in your trunk. You never know when you'll need one or the other or both.

Don't give advice if they don't ask for it.

● ● ●

Buy the healthiest dog food. Any animal that's as unconditionally loving as they are, needs and deserves only the best.

● ● ●

Get good at visualizing and 'thinking from the end.' We live in a very feeling-oriented world. Feeling good equals attracting good.

● ● ●

Never pour oatmeal down your sister's shirt. That's also mean if you stop and think about it.

When you're off to buy a car,
make sure dependability and gas
mileage are among the top priorities.

* * *

Travel cross country but drive, don't fly. And
take the back roads if you're in no hurry.
Expressways are boring.

* * *

Rearrange your room.

* * *

Since we are a country that spends lots of
time around our refrigerators, hang sacred
stuff on the door. At least we can feel good
before putting on the extra calories.

Training with partners is great
but now and again, train alone.
It's good for mental toughness.

● ● ●

Remember: You have to have the bricks
before you can build the house. True in
writing, true in life.

● ● ●

'Raining cats and dogs', 'the whole nine
yards', 'knock on wood': If you get bored,
google where sayings like these came from.
It's pretty fascinating.

Even if your superstitions are quirky and bordering on ridiculous, if you believe in them, stick with them. You don't have to explain to anyone.

● ● ●

Don't always let your boss win.
Sometimes it's good to let them know you have it within you to be your own boss one day.

● ● ●

Have your cake, cut it, and eat it, too.
It's your cake, right?

Appreciate the kind of friends who you can
be around and not have to say a word.
Ironically, there's a lot to be 'said' for that.

● ● ●

If you're a football fan, appreciate the
effectiveness of the simple slant pattern.

● ● ●

And please explain to me the 'delayed draw'
on 3rd-and-1. Why you want to make a guy
gain seven yards just to gain one is way
beyond me.

Don't just fall in love with nature,
learn from it. It's where nothing is forced, yet
everything gets done at just the perfect time.

● ● ●

Avoid hurrying. It ends up taking more time.

● ● ●

When submitting a word document,
a social media post, or an important email,
ALWAYS read over it one more time
before hitting 'send.'

● ● ●

And be careful before you hit 'reply to all.'
Many times, 'all' don't want to hear it.

If you're into losing weight, avoid big dinners. Eating big, then going to sleep may not be the best game plan.

● ● ●

Avoid all those monster fuel and energy drinks. They may keep you awake for a month but they're not very good for you.

● ● ●

Before getting on I-16 between Macon and Savannah, make dang sure you are wide awake. By the time you hit Soperton, you probably won't be.

When involved in a financial transaction, if the people you're doing business with are rude, take it somewhere else if you can. Don't give your money to people you don't like.

● ● ●

To keep your mind active, take up crossword puzzles, word jumbles, sudokus, and jigsaw puzzles. And work on learning people's names.

● ● ●

Never get behind a microphone after a good drink or a long run.

When packing a gym bag, don't forget your socks. Running in argyles makes you look like one weird boy.

* * *

Don't fall in love with desserts or soft drinks. Both enjoy making your stomach large.

* * *

Never heckle a beginning comedian. That's a hard life; try it sometime!

* * *

Dream big, and if you're not enjoying the journey, then consider changing the dream.

If want to be a writer, keep this rule in mind:
You can do anything you want when you
write…as long as you do it well.

● ● ●

Never snoop in your sister's room and read
her diary. On second thought, why not just
leave your sister alone?

● ● ●

Get to know a hockey referee.
They have all kinds of interesting stories –
most of them true.

If you ever attend a camp as a coach, spend at least one of the nights in the after-hours hospitality room. Speaking of good stories…

• • •

Have as many conversations with your grandparents as you can. There's simply no replacement for their experiences and wisdom.

• • •

Loving who you're around and what you're doing almost always makes up for your lack of knowledge. Unless you work for NASA, you can learn what's needed on the fly.

When you're packing,
don't forget your cell phone charger.
Then again, maybe you should…

● ● ●

Play the stocks but don't let them rule or
dictate your life.

● ● ●

To make yourself commit to fitness,
pay the entry fee of a race or event way ahead
of time. Something about money that makes a
person move.

And pack your pillowcase if you're in a hotel
the night before the big event.
Something about the smell of your own
pillow that helps you sleep better.

• • •

Have someone look over your written words
or speech, but in the end, make sure the
finished product comes from YOUR heart,
not theirs.

• • •

Develop the art and wisdom of saying
absolutely nothing at all.

Never ask a bald headed guy if you can borrow his hairbrush. Some of them don't like that very much.

● ● ●

If you think the devil's fiddle is better than Johnny's in the song "The Devil Went Down to Georgia," keep it to yourself. Some people find that sacra-religious.

● ● ●

Whatever the stress, whatever the mess, whatever the injury, whatever the problem, sometimes there's simply nothing better to do for it than get a good night's sleep.

When escorting your date or daughter to midfield at homecoming, make sure your fly is zipped up. Otherwise, the ensuing pictures will be terribly embarrassing.

* * *

At the beginning of each day, go forth remembering the 11th Commandment: Thou Shalt Not Be a Jerk.

* * *

Share the planet.

On Mother's and Father's Day,
don't just reach out to your own parent,
connect with as many as possible. Being a
parent is the most underrated job EVER.

● ● ●

Remember: Kid's don't come with a manual.
Spend lots of time listening and observing,
not just talking.

● ● ●

A coaching wisdom: Sometimes knowing
when to shut up is just as important as
knowing what to say.

Never swat a fly that's resting on top of your
favorite white shirt.

* * *

Fall in love with green tea.
Personally, I hate the taste, but the benefits of
that stuff are many and plenty.

* * *

Every now and again, write in passive voice
and/or start a sentence with a preposition. But
if your English teachers asks, you did NOT
hear this from me.

In a heated group argument, keep your eyes on the one who gets quiet all of a sudden. That's the one who often blows things up.

● ● ●

When resigning from a bad work situation, tell your boss "you've found a better opportunity" rather than rip the existing job. At some point, you'll be glad you did.

● ● ●

In the long run, the only person you consistently have to be better than is the person you were the day before.

You are right, life isn't fair! In the long run it's actually weighted in your favor.

● ● ●

Remember, in some countries burping at the table is a compliment to the chef.
Not exactly true in America.

● ● ●

When your girlfriend asks for corrections in life or in appearance, be VERY careful when suggesting improvements.

● ● ●

If you screw this up, see above wisdom about the joys and freedoms of sleeping on your couch. You may be there for a while.

Never bring up a new subject when someone is about to write you a check. Leave them in their current train of thought.

● ● ●

Even if your office space, dorm room, or home is filled with inspirational quotes, swap them out every month or so. Fresh room equals fresh mind.

● ● ●

Start your own quote book – Extraordinary Quotes from Ordinary People. Ordinary people say just as neat stuff as famous people – why shouldn't they get the love?

Be wary when new people join you at various
stages when you're having a meal.
That's usually when you end up
eating way too much.

* * *

When at a convention or conference, get in
conversations with the attendees as well as
the presenters. You can learn a lot from both.

* * *

Lead, follow, or get out of the way, and
quickly learn what each situation calls for.

* * *

Live your life where you simply
can't wait for karma to kick in.

Listen to the lyrics of Jackson Browne and
John Denver songs, but don't expect that to
necessarily make you a chick magnet.

● ● ●

If you fail at what you are passion about,
remember this is where the story begins, not
where it ends! Abe Lincoln lost 12 straight
elections before winning the presidency.

● ● ●

Never go into a place where mixed
martial arts fighting is on every TV.
It won't be long before all will be chaos
in the audience as well.

They say your biggest regret in life will be
what you don't do. I contend the worst
thing will be NOT being yourself
while you are down here.

* * *

Stop cracking on your exes and - even if it
was their fault - forgive them, not necessarily
because they deserve it, but because YOU do.

* * *

Whether in sports or in life, start from where
you are, not where you think you should be.

Appreciate the macho football players of the world but get to know the cross country runners as well. They have feelings, too.

● ● ●

Don't get carried away when watching college football. They are just kids, and they're doing the best they can! (Right, like I'm actually going to take that advice!)

● ● ●

It's not what you do, it's how you do it.

● ● ●

Get yourself a heating pad.
Those things are underrated.

187

Never underestimate the intelligence of a Starbucks employee. With as many variations of drinks there are, they have to be rather smart just to work there.

❀ ❀ ❀

When you need to remember something, write it on your hand. Notes get lost, tying a string around your finger may not work. Your hand, though, isn't going anywhere.

❀ ❀ ❀

When a good friend asks for advice, be honest even if it hurts. If he turns to hit you, then run away. Actually, he will appreciate the advice and you in the end.

Every now and then, read a book from the
Young Adult section.

● ● ●

Never forget: this world isn't nearly as bad as
the media makes it out to be. There are a lot
of good people, places, and events out there.

● ● ●

A friend in need is a friend indeed works two
ways. They need you when they're down but
uplift them in their joys as well. Otherwise,
you're just misery loves company.

If the place you're in doesn't have Wi-Fi, good! Call your mom, compose a letter, read a book, talk to a stranger. Interface in person!

❂ ❂ ❂

Find or start a good support group.

❂ ❂ ❂

When someone loses a loved one, reach out to them at some point. You may not think your efforts matter, but they do.

❂ ❂ ❂

If you ever start to feel like a worthless piece of crap, remember you're here for a reason. God doesn't make mistakes! (Except when he invented roaches.)

Look people in the eye when you're talking to them … unless they're not genuine. In that case, look wherever you want to, then move on.

● ● ●

Be nice – unless someone's trying to hack into your social media or bank accounts.
In that case, let them have it with both barrels. Make it up to God later.

● ● ●

If you start making a truckload of money and living the life of your dreams, keep it to yourself. Why attract jealousy when you don't have to?

After a good workout, use ice for swelling but otherwise, stick with heat.

● ● ●

Never try to make butter stick to the ceiling when at the dinner table. Neither moms nor dads tend to like that very much.

● ● ●

At least once in your life,
sleep outside or in a tree house.

● ● ●

And participate in some type of march or walk that's for a good cause.

If you own one cat, do your homework before getting another one. That doesn't always work out very well.

* * *

If you're in a hurricane, remember there's as much danger in the aftermath as in the storm itself.

* * *

When going to a boxing match, remember that a front row seat is not necessarily a good thing.

* * *

If you get involved in a significant money transaction, put it in writing.

At graduation, always comply when a grad
wants to have a picture taken with you.
Consider it an honor… because it is.

● ● ●

View yourself as no better and no worse than
everyone you meet.

● ● ●

And no matter how good you think you are
at something, there's always someone better.

● ● ●

Hobbies are great but find at least one thing
in life that you dive into with reckless
abandon. Learn what you can about it and
then, learn some more.

Learn to ask for signs from the Heavens,
and don't forget to give thanks
when you get them.

● ● ●

Always ask before putting ketchup
on the basket of fries.

● ● ●

Even if you disagree, at least hear their side of
the story. You'll at least learn where they're
coming from, and maybe even what they've
been through.

● ● ●

Keep your wallet, keys,
and cell phone in the same place.

Keep Drano under your bathroom sink.

* * *

Never talk about how pretty other women are when you're with your girlfriend. This does NOT make you attractive yourself.

* * *

If someone takes a swing at you, duck or get out of the way. You also knew that, right?

* * *

Fearing death is understandable, but fearing life is worse – much worse.

Whether you're generous, a tightwad,
or somewhere in between,
pick up a tab every now and then.

❂ ❂ ❂

Find a car repair shop that doesn't suggest
excessive repairs every time you get the oil
changed. When you find one you trust,
recommend them to your friends.

❂ ❂ ❂

Even if it's a small fender bender, unless you
know and trust the person call the police.

❂ ❂ ❂

Never do it later if you can do it now.
Other things do come up.

197

If you're a college student, handling distractions will perhaps be the toughest thing you have to learn. After all, they will appear everywhere. And most every night.

● ● ●

Whether in your job or your marriage, remember that if you don't work at it, it will eventually go away.

● ● ●

Whether waiting tables or playing sports - and whether you're good or bad - always hustle. People will respect that as much or more than your talent.

If you teach something, remember this philosophy: They hear; therefore they yawn. But when they do, then they know.

● ● ●

Never underestimate the power of a simple smile.

● ● ●

Instead of constantly lecturing, every now and again put your hand on your kids' shoulders, look them in the eye, and simply let them know you're on their side.

This seemingly simple gesture from my father changed everything – and for the better. In fact, I have goosebumps just writing this.

● ● ●

Make sure you compete where –
at the end of the day when looking back on it
– you smile because you did all you could,
when you could.

● ● ●

And you won't sleep well if you don't.

● ● ●

Never send a text or email at three in the morning. I mean, go to sleep!

Put a screensaver photo on your computer
that elicits a smile times twelve.
You deserve to feel good while you're
evolving through life.

● ● ●

In the professional world, make time for
people even when they are NOT
writing you a check.

● ● ●

Don't shy away from taking credit, but don't
seek it out either.

● ● ●

Speak right, travel light, write tight, and keep
your goals in sight.

While important to be honest with others, always be honest with yourself as well. It saves lots of time and lots of trouble.

● ● ●

Find a career that allows you to use your gifts to their maximum capacities.

● ● ●

Pray with your feet moving.

● ● ●

At least once a year, wash your blue jeans whether they need it or not.

In tennis – particularly in doubles –
serve into the body.

● ● ●

In basketball, be aggressive right from the
opening tip. This sets the tone not only for the
game, but with the officials as well.

● ● ●

Learn how to read the body languages of the
people you work with.

● ● ●

If you're broke, tell your friends beforehand
you won't be buying them Christmas gifts.
They will not only understand, they might
even buy you lunch.

It's not how you start; it's how you finish.

● ● ●

Don't kick a man when he's down,
but don't kick him when he's up, either.
Tend to your own garden.

● ● ●

Remember: There is a such thing as justice.
Unfortunately, it often takes a lot longer than
you want it to.

● ● ●

Every now and then, check for ticks. Those
little bastards can cause LOTS of trouble!

Speak at someone's funeral. It's a tough, but powerful thing to do.

● ● ●

Write your own eulogy but leave out the part where you fell through the roof of your own school.

● ● ●

Invent a breathalyzer that knocks people off social media when they've had too much. You'll become a trillionaire and you will have deserved every penny.

● ● ●

Have a pregame ritual and stick to it.

Be wary of roommates who
enjoy lighting their farts.

* * *

And be wary of rattlesnakes.
I mean, they're poisonous, right?

* * *

Keep your phone and
your computer charged.

* * *

Notice the body language of your date when
she's in the passenger seat. If she's practically
falling out her window, at least enjoy the
conversation.

When you start work, remember that
spiritual values are as important in the
professional environment as anywhere else.
Jerks need not apply.

● ● ●

Pay for the lady's dinner on a date,
but never pick up the tab if you're out with a
bunch of freeloaders.

● ● ●

Remember: "Think long think wrong" might
be a good poker saying, but "think again"
might be the right saying if you're about to
jump off a cliff. Or buying a boat.

Don't just congratulate an artist, writer, or athlete, find out how they trained and prepared. Pick their brains about how they did what they did and why.

* * *

Remember: A lot goes on after midnight and a lot of it is not good. Get some sleep.

* * *

When you're sleep deprived,
you won't think as well, test as well,
perform as well, talk yourself out of trouble
as well, or even flirt as well. Enough said.

Don't you ever quit. Unless it's smoking, drinking or all those other bad habits.

● ● ●

Learning the rules and regulations are fine, but don't be afraid to throw some "you" into everything you do. That's why God put you down here.

● ● ●

Smile! The year 2020 has been tough in a lot of ways, but it's almost over.

Whatever your religion, make sure it preaches kindness – and has nothing against coffee with cream and teeth-rotting amounts of sugar.

* * *

Pass this book on! If you didn't enjoy the read, at least it'll make a great coaster for your coffee table.

* * *

And be nice to everyone you meet…including your little sister. This world will function a lot better when there's more love around.

All Said & Dunn

Thanks for listening, reading, joining me on what has been a great adventure. If you don't agree with all these, I get it. Personally, I never read my books once they're published – I know I'll find something and cringe, see a mistake, wonder why the heck I said what I said.

I've always found it easier just to close the book. Move on. Be done with it.

Still, pass this on. To your kids. Your spouse. Your boss. Or how about this: Jot your own down while charting your own course, celebrating your own victories and crying over your own losses.

We are a society that studies history, but we don't learn from it. Don't make that mistake. By putting pen to paper, things go deeper into your brain. I either read that somewhere or I just made it up. Still, when something is written it becomes a thing. It's out there, it's real.

Personally, I like to think big. Write one of these books and leave it for your grandchildren. Don't wait until they graduate, don't wait for anything. Let them benefit from what moved you, what made you get up each morning, and what you thought about when you went to bed.

It's funny, we live in a world where we divide ourselves up SO much. North, south, east, west, white, black, southern, northern, foreign, left handed, right handed, democrat, republican. I choose to buy into none of it.

We're all human. We want to love and be loved. We want to matter. We want to contribute. Perhaps my worst moments in life weren't about wins and losses, or even getting dumped by my wife, it was the thought that I was NOT making a difference while here.

I can handle winning. And losing. And even the girl saying no. But being on this planet and making zero effect? Not an option.

So, make your effect. Or, like one of these bullet points above said, don't just go with the flow, create it. We live in crazy times; we need good people breaking out the oars right now. We need it bad.

Break them out in peace. Pass along your wisdom. Pass along hope.

But never, I mean never, forget to laugh. After all, I can't help but thinking that God has a great sense of humor, and I can't help but think he wants us to enjoy this earth trip.

Enough from me. Thanks again. And God Bless.

About the Author

Dunn Neugebauer is living an adventurous life – he's sold cookware door to door, worked the cash register at McDonalds, officiated at a national championship flag football tournament with no credentials, worked at a bank (sort of), taught tennis, written sports for newspapers, and coached tennis to people of all shapes and sizes. He has two other books available on Amazon – 'Funny Conversations with God' and 'Rock Bottom, Then Up Again.' Currently, he works at a school in Atlanta where he does carpool, writes for the communication department, coaches cross country and track, subs in the Upper School and actually likes it, and collects and writes sports stories at night before hitting the bed. He also pens a "Slices of Life" blog on Facebook and has written two novels, though he prefers not to talk about either of them. Please know – in successes and in failures - that he means well.